IT'S PLAYTIME!

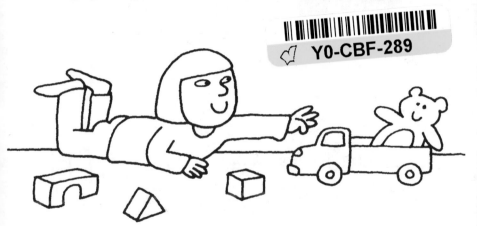

by Don L. Curry
Illustrated by Mavis Smith

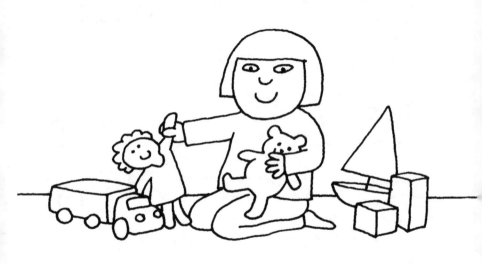

It's playtime!

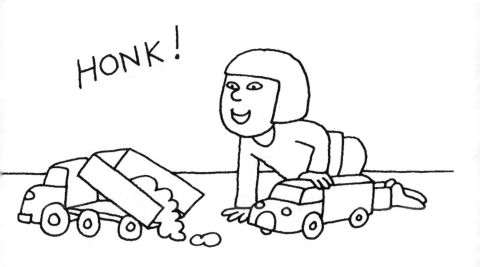

I play with trucks.

3

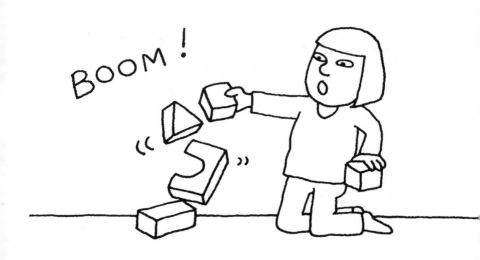

I play with blocks.

4

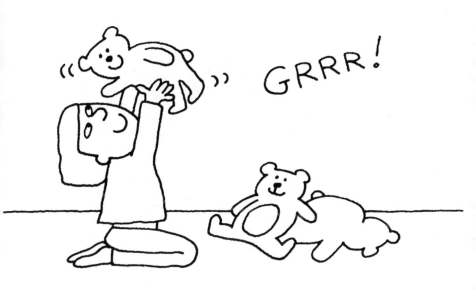

I play with teddy bears.

5

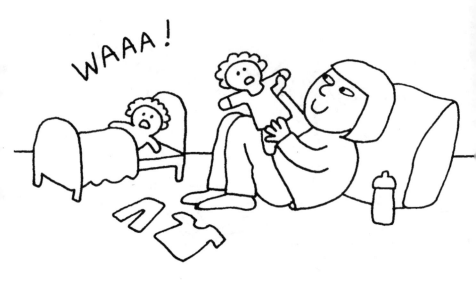

I play with dolls.

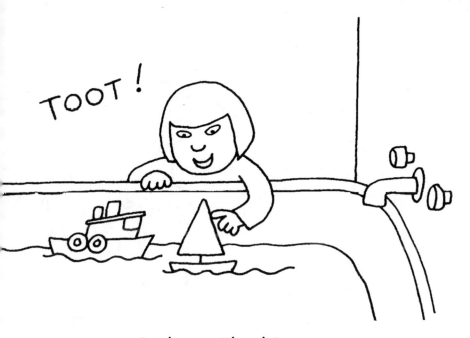

I play with ships.

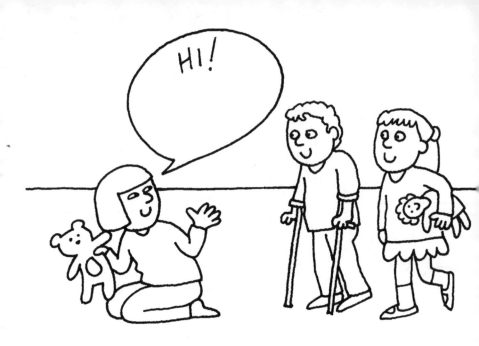

I play with friends.